TIGHT
CORNER

TIGHT CORNER

by KEN GRUNDY & MALCOLM WILLETT

Andrews and McMeel
A Universal Press Syndicate Company
Kansas City

ISBN: 0-8362-0422-0

Library of Congress Catalog Card Number: 95-77576

"You know ... I can't remember
what I did yesterday."

Olympic All-Arounder.

The return of the legendary
Homing Tortoise.

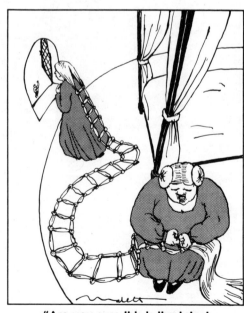

"Are you sure this is the latest
fashion, Rapunzel?"

Malcolm's highwayman days
came abruptly to an end after he
had worked all day in the sun.

Making the rounds of the
infectious diseases wing.

"We first met at a resuscitation class."

The last words from the world's
worst accountant.

A classic performance from Jimi Hendrix

Mrs. Lake conquers agoraphobia.

"Ha! Ha! We've stopped sinking! We're gonna be all right, Shorty!... Shorty?"

"OK, so it's not that one. When you say 'right a bit,' is that your right or from the street right?"

"Let me through ... I'm a filing clerk."

Possums playing.

"I think he wants something
a little heavier."

Helium salesman.

"The defendant will rise. The jury
has reached a unanimous
decision: What is guilt?"

11

"It sure beats regurgitation."

The couch potato's whole life flashed before him.

"You boys been following
that star again?"

3 a.m., and the Olympic Synchronized
Car-Door-Slamming Team
is still practicing.

"Payday, Chief! Second rank back, fifth
from the left ... rheumatoid arthritis."

"Mummy will be back soon ... I know!
Let's play 'This Little Piggy' again."

"... and the last thing I remember was the great storm of '64."

"OK! OK! If this doesn't work, we'll try your idea."

CALL THIS A ROMANTIC CRUISE FOR TWO?!

"I've seen the X-rays, Mr. Mergatroyd, and the leg has to come off, the sooner the better. Certainly by Sunday lunchtime."

The second you find yourself on the endangered species list, a car backfires!

Across a crowded room, their eyes met.

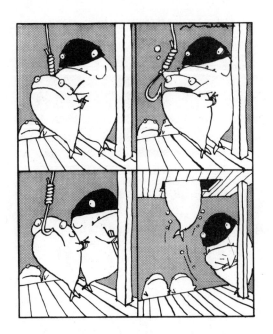

Scientists discover the end
of the universe.

"I now pronounce this animal d...
Wait for it! Wait for it!"

Houdini — the early years.

"Presentation, Maurice, presentation."

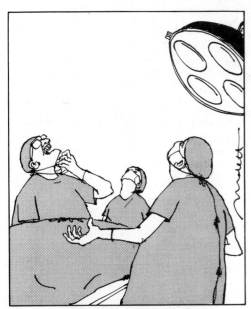

"Now, that's what I call a
donor heart rejection!"

"Take 348 and ACTION!"

Marriage in the Germ Research Labs.

The modern male.

"It's not a pretty sight. He was in the water for a long time."

Miss Kumbria has trouble with her stiletto heels on the escalator.

"Your references are impeccable, but I'm afraid you're overqualified."

"Put some of this on, Honey. ... You're crackling."

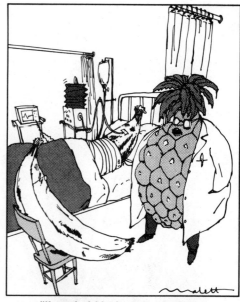

"I'm afraid he's going to be a
vegetable for the rest of his life."

Herbert finds the first meeting of the
Levitation Society empty.

The successful man-eater first gains
their confidence.

Houdini paints the only way he knows how.

"Wonderful! Just wonderful! I'm tired, cold, hungry, and now it starts to evaporate!"

"Come on, everybody, it's midnight.
Unmask! Unmask!"

"Congratulations, Signor Banano,
your plans for the tower have
been accepted."

"Half a dozen Grade A, wasn't it?"

Having put his shoes on the wrong feet,
Col. Harris refuses to take no for
an answer.

Michelangelo (6½) starts well, but his
concentration wanders.

Mr. Whitliff, CIA (Ret.), finds old
habits die hard.

"Allow me to draw your attention to paragraph three — the 'spontaneous combustion' clause."

Sunday morning with the Invisibles.

Yes, the whole world
has gone mad.

"How are these? Better?"

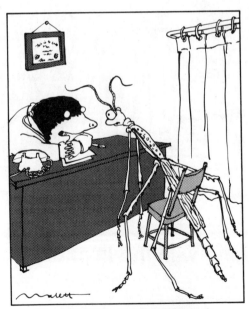

"I've seen the results of the tests,
and you haven't got anorexia ...
you're a stick insect!"

"Dad, the Tooth Fairy came! ... At least that's who he said he was."

Accountant Hugh Lask's secret desire doesn't interfere with his daily work.

"Welcome to the 14th reunion of the Humans Raised by Animals Society."

"I don't know how this place gets into such a mess, I really don't."

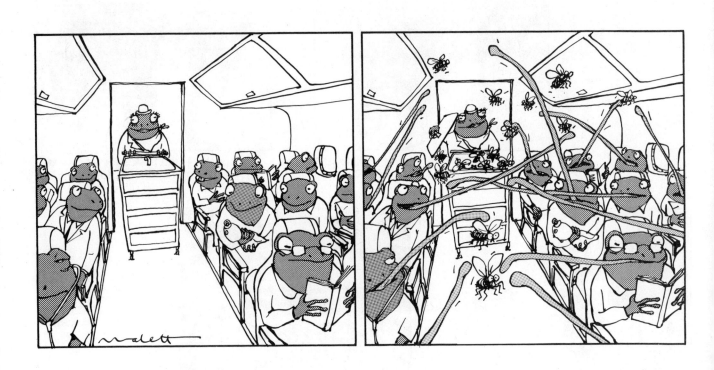

"Status symbol? No, no, it just gets me from A to B."

"So much for parental guidance!"

Solitary confinement.

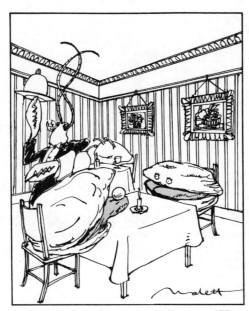

"For me? And you made it yourself!"

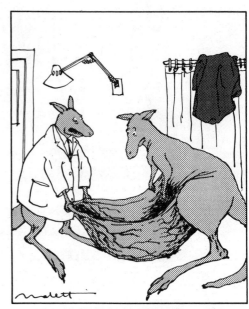

"It looks like Baby Sitter's Pouch."

"I told you before, kid! You ain't got that kinda dough."

High-tech animal training.

"Happy, darling?"

"Cathy, I do wonder about that boy. That's the
eighth glass of water he's wanted tonight."

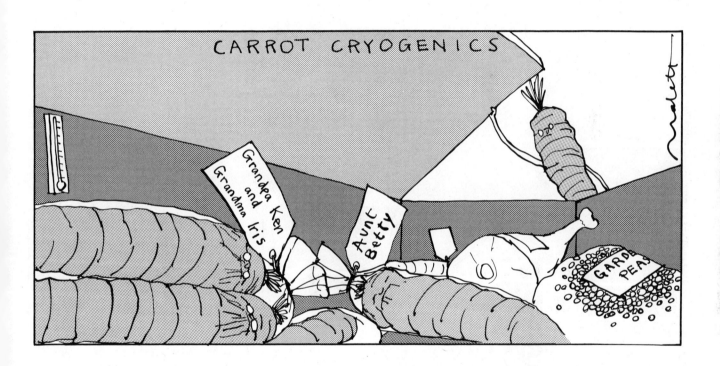

Mr. Donahue's left foot goes to sleep.

During the horror movie,
Bobby inks himself.

Kevin feeds his face.

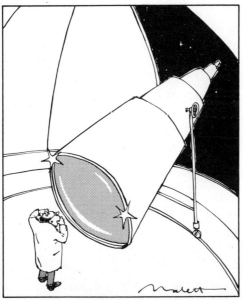

Unknown to Bradford, the cleaning lady
holds the answer as to why the universe
has expanded 800,000 times overnight.

"... and for stealing all the horses
in this here county!"

"Oh what! Out all evening, and no
one tells me I've got something
in my teeth."

"Take three of these pills a day. They're specially formulated to suppress the appetite."

"You can see why I'm always broke. This is only one week's worth of deodorant."

The town where all the
good guys get killed.

"Hansel and Gretel" for the '90s.

"Ready, Barbara? 10, 9, 8, 7 ..."

"How much for the bucket
of sand?"

The Siamese Twins Club dinner,
first sitting.

"When can you start?"

The Frankenstein School
of Architecture.

"Mommy, how many stuffed animals
had to die to make that?"

"I hate it when this thing gets stuck in the tunnel."

"You've still got your safety catch on."

"Nurse, I think the ventilator's turned up a little high."

"I dunno, Brad ... I thought it would be more technical."

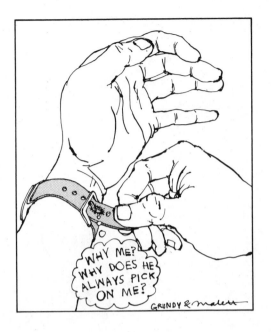

"Good Sir Knight, I hear the rainy season has started in your kingdom."

"Kevin Chameleon! That's the *fourth* time you've gone red!"

"Have I died and gone to heaven?"

"Don't make any sudden moves, Barry,
but I think you've got my clothes on."

48

After four days without food, being adrift with the catering crew somehow made it tougher.

**Henry decides his psychiatrist
may be underqualified.**

**Theater critic for *Guns and Ammo*
magazine.**

What lazy lumberjacks dream.

"You know, Peters, if only all civilizations made hieroglyphics this legible, it would save chaps like us a lot of grief."

"Darling, you simply must try the Canada goose."

Night falls hard in Watertown, Conn.

"Yes, that's my husband. He's always
a bit shy at parties."

"Come along, you two. Haven't you got homes to go to?"

"Now you can howl at the sun!"

"... and the task tonight is to create heaven and earth. Our present champion holds the record at six days."

"That's Frank, bless him, overworked at the slaughterhouse again."

"624 Squadron ... scramble!"

"Now, try it with this one."

High-tech Hell.

The **first** model T Ford mass-production line.

Mobile librarians.

"Have your wife shoot one of these into your rump, three times a day."

"OK, OK, you win. The blue ones are nicer — fire the pretty blue ones."

"I had my sentence cut, but do I get a
visit from my other half? Heck, no!"

"It's a .35 Winchester repeating rifle, semiautomatic
reload, 12 rounds, range 600 yards. Or, as the
gentleman so nicely put it, a 'bang-stick'!"

Fate's double whammy.

"Mom, which sun oil should I use ...
rare, medium or well-done?"

"I'd like to make a complaint. There are no complimentary mice in my room."

Christmas dinner with the bomb disposal squad.

"Next time, *you* keep them talking while *I* do the stealing."

Jake's "you could hear a pin drop"
entrance was ruined. He wished he hadn't
shot the piano player the week before.

"Spread it around! They'll be here
any minute, and I can't let them
see the place like this."

The Hollywood set-builder
arrives home.

"I dealt, gentlemen. Mr. Smee
to open, I believe."

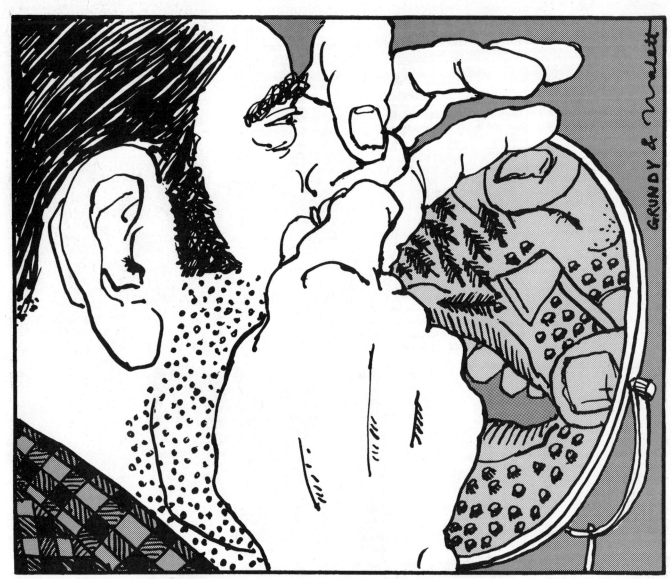

Bob was every inch a lumberjack.

"Look, darling! Don't you think that pair of legs would suit Melissa and me down to the ground?"

"They match, chief. I'll have him picked up."

Within two weeks of the moon being colonized.

Not smoking behind the bike shed.

Al finally finds a bar where he can commission the perfect murder.

The Tooth Fairy shows off
her new acquisition.

"This is our top of the line."

"I like you, Maurice — you ain't like the
rest. Pity the cattle drive ends in Tombstone
tomorrow. Heck, I'm gonna miss you."

"Tell us what we want to know, and
the antiperspirant's all yours."

"Other guys get beer bellies. I get a beer brow."

"Lighten up! They can't keep the beaches closed forever."

Lost in the mists of time: how "Stonewall" Jackson really got his nickname.

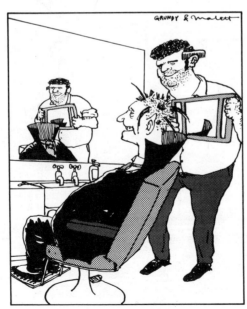

"Err ... lovely, thank you."

"This new captain makes the mornings just fly by."

"And again! This time with more feeling!"

"Could you sign our petition for improved working conditions?"

Luckily, it was discovered that brain surgeon P. Lange was raving mad *before* he attempted his new "rapid skull entry" technique.

"No problem, captain. I've got a spare for this model."

The ever-changing world of fashion.

The sad reality of tranquilizer-dart addiction.

Why lightning never strikes twice in the same place.

"Can't talk now, Helen. I've got to take the kids to school."

"Shoot! I thought you guys were vegetarians."

The Minotaur: half man, all bull.

"... and this pair are perfect to wear on vacation —
they speak Spanish!"

"We're hoping she'll grow up to be a plastic surgeon."

Translation: "Got to go, honey.
People are waiting."

"Go and annoy your father. Can't
you see he's in a good mood?"

"I'm not so sure about this
circus exchange idea."

The long-awaited separation of the
Siamese twins joined at the eyebrows.

"OK, Pinky, round 'em up, boy!"

"Look what I found under Junior's bed!"

Olympics for people with
low self-esteem.

20,000 years ago, the tribe that invented nuclear-tipped arrows starved to death.

"... and if he sniffs out anything, we reward him with a juicy bone."

"You're squeezing again!"

"I'll say this for Morrie: He knows how to fleece a tourist!"

Superman, age 89, unable to leap tall
buildings in a single bound.

During the great ball boy strike of '76.

Marking exam papers in ESP.

The Human Cannonball discharges
himself from the hospital.

432 light-years from Earth,
we witness the death of a star.

Eleventh finger, 28th hand. That's where
he placed the wedding band.

"Martha, I think this candlelit dinner for two may have been a mistake."

Operating on the Invisible Man.

"I don't care what you do, just get me some more ice."

"You're wearing that electric cattle prod mighty low, stranger."

Garlic breath.

King Kong was a nasty kid.

"If you need anything, just scream
until your lungs drop out."

"Tell me if I'm pressing too hard."

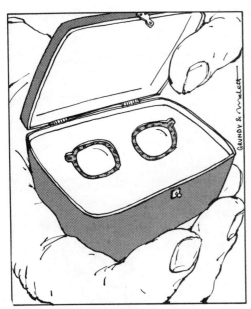

Contact lenses for that
intellectual look.

Underwater protection racket.

The country singer's wife changed a
light bulb, and for four hours he sang
about how good the old one was.

After 14 years and $8 billion, scientists
discover the building blocks of life itself.

"It's actually true for once! Your son isn't overweight; he's just big-boned."